WHO WOULD WIN?

ULTIMATE SHOWDOWN

5 BOOKS IN 1!

BY
JERRY PALLOTTA

ILLUSTRATED BY
ROB BOLSTER

📖 SCHOLASTIC

The publisher would like to thank the following for their
kind permission to use their photographs in this book:

Photos ©: cover center: logolord/Shutterstock; cover textures: Andrey_Kuzmin/Shutterstock and Kompaniets Taras/
Shutterstock; 1: logolord/Shutterstock; 8: Andy Rouse/NHPA/Photoshot; 9: Thomas Mangelsen/Minden Pictures; 18: J & C
Sohns/age fotostock; 19: Marc Moritsch/National Geographic Creative; 22: Michel & Christine Denis-Huot/Biosphoto; 23: Anup
Shah/Photodisc/Getty Images; 24: Andy Rouse/NHPA/Photoshot; 25: Renee Lynn/Corbis/VCG/Getty Images; 38, 39: Norbert Wu;
40: Chris Newbert/Minden Pictures; 41: Franco Banfi/WaterF/age fotostock; 54 bottom: Azure Computer & Photo Srvs/Animals
Animals; 55 top: Image Quest Marine; 55 center: Seapics; 55 bottom: Brandon Cole Marine Photography; 76: John Warden/
AlaskaStock.com; 77: Gunther Matschke/AlaskaStock.com; 82: Courtesy of Dave Newbury/Dept. Of Anatomy/University of
Bristol; 83: Courtesy of Cooper Landing Museum; 84: Agami Photo Agency/Dreamstime; 85: Michio Hoshino/Minden Pictures;
103 top: florintt/iStockphoto; 108 center: Alastair Macewen/Getty Images; 110 center: Biophoto Assoc./Science Source; 115
bottom: Kent Dannen/Science Source; 116 top: Staff Sgt. Andy M. Kin/Department of Defense; 116 bottom: Courtesy of
Sacramento State; 117 top: Mass Communication Specialist 2nd Class Zachary L. Borden/U.S. Navy; 117 bottom left: Courtesy
of London Wasps; 117 bottom right: Hirz/Getty Images; 128: Ulrich Joger from an expedition sponsored by the Braunschweig
(Germany) National History Museum in Niger, 2006; 129: Nigel Roddis/Reuters; 136: The Natural History Museum/The Image
Works; 137: Xinhua/Alamy Stock Photo; 142 top: xijian/iStockphoto; 143 top: Mengzhang/Dreamstime; 143 bottom right: Tim
Evanson/Flickr with permission from Jack Horner, Museum of the Rockies.

Thank you to my research assistants, Olivia Packenham and Will Harney. Also, thank you to author
and zoo guy Roland Smith.
To cousin Jeanne Petronio, who comes from the hammerhead side of the family.
Thank you to my research assistants, Olivia Packenham and Will Harney. And thank you to author
Shelley Gill for a zillion bear stories.
Thank you to beekeepers Rosie and Jim Lonborg, American League Cy Young award winner, 1967.
To my two new pals, Sloane and Shane!

—*J.P.*

To Eddie.
To my "Running Bear," Luke.
Thank you to N.C. Wyeth.
Thank you to my beloved mother and grandmother for always encouraging me to draw!

—*R.B.*

-TABLE of CONTENTS-

WHO WOULD WIN?

LION VS. TIGER

What would happen if a lion and a tiger met each other? What if they were both hungry? What if these two big cats had a fight? Who do you think would win?

Meet the lion. Lions are mammals. Their fur is one solid color—tan, brown, or dark tan. They have no stripes or spots on their fur. Lions have an unforgettable face.

SCIENTIFIC NAME OF TIGER
"Panthera tigris"

Meet the tiger. Tigers are mammals too! Tigers are orange or rust-colored with black stripes. Underneath their soft fur is lots of muscle.

AFRICA

These two big cats live mostly on different continents. Almost all lions live in Africa. A few lions can be found in the Gir Forest of India, in Asia.

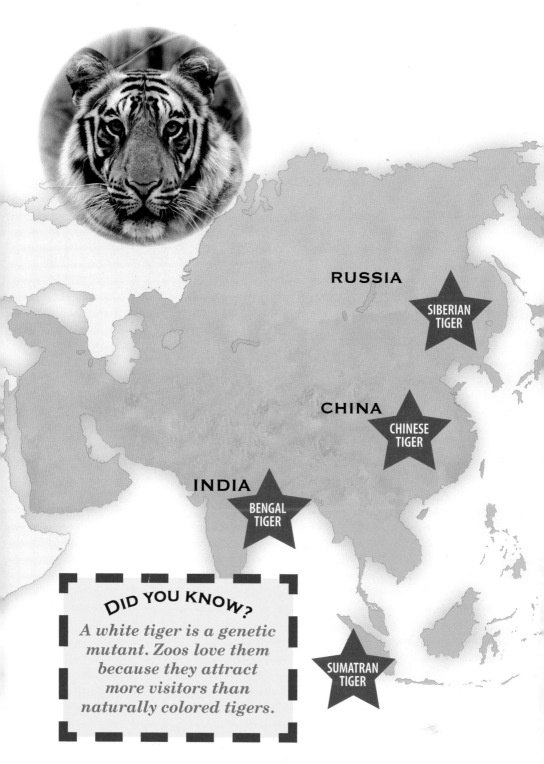

RUSSIA

SIBERIAN TIGER

CHINA

CHINESE TIGER

INDIA

BENGAL TIGER

SUMATRAN TIGER

DID YOU KNOW?

A white tiger is a genetic mutant. Zoos love them because they attract more visitors than naturally colored tigers.

Tigers live in many parts of Asia. The largest tiger is the Siberian, or Amur, tiger.

Lions prefer to live on open, grassy plains.

Bonus Fact

A grassy plain is a perfect place for a lion to live. Lions mostly eat animals that graze on grass.

Tigers prefer to live in thick woods and rain forests.

Lions have huge, strong jaws. They have sharp teeth for cutting and tearing. The long canine teeth allow lions to hold on to an animal after they catch it.

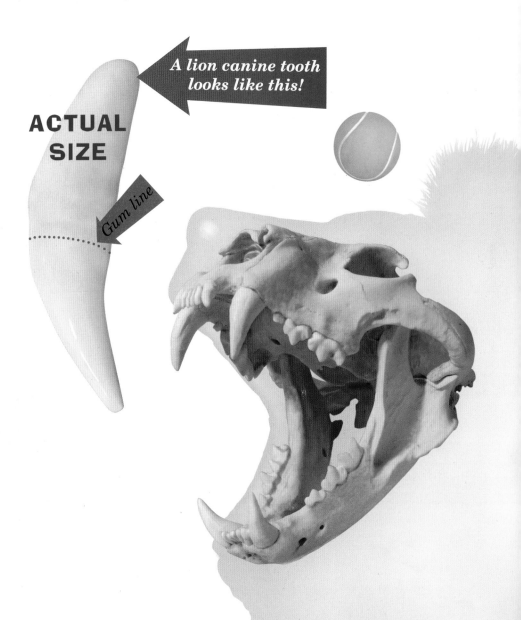

A lion canine tooth looks like this!

ACTUAL SIZE

Gum line

Lions have a big skull. But their brain is small, about the size of a tennis ball. Lions are not considered very smart.

Tigers also have a large skull, but their brain is only as big as a baseball. A small brain usually means that an animal is not smart. However, zookeepers have found tigers to be intelligent.

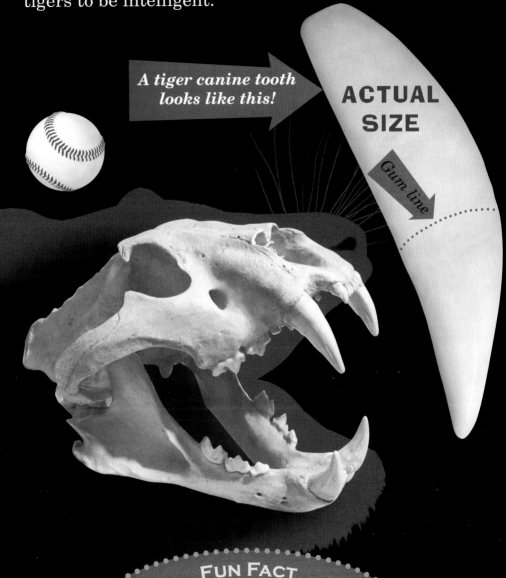

A tiger canine tooth looks like this!

ACTUAL SIZE

Gum line

FUN FACT
House cats have teeth just like a tiger. The last tooth in the top jaw of every cat—even your pet cat—goes sideways.

Animals a lion eats

GIRAFFE

ELEPHANT

HIPPOPOTAMUS

CAPE BUFFALO

ZEBRA

WILDEBEEST

SPRINGBOK

BABOON

REMEMBER

"Eyes in front, like to hunt."
"Eyes on side, like to hide."

Lions are carnivores—they eat meat. They don't go to the supermarket or a restaurant. Lions are predators that hunt, catch, and eat other animals.

MOOSE

DEER

COW

BEAR

WILD BOAR

RABBIT

DID YOU KNOW?

OMNIVORES
eat everything

HERBIVORES
eat plants

CARNIVORES
eat meat

INSECTIVORES
eat insects

Tigers are also carnivores. They stalk, kill, and eat other animals. Tigers are clever and creative when hunting their prey.

Most of the time, lionesses do the hunting. They hunt in teams. The big male lions stay back and protect the cubs from attack.

Tigers usually hunt at night. Males and females each hunt alone. Tigers are sneakier than lions.

INTERESTING FACT

Hunters who go after tigers sometimes discover that the tiger is hunting *them*.

The male lion is the one with the big fuzzy mane around his neck. Female lions, or lionesses, have no manes.

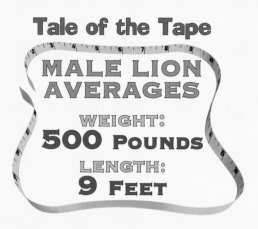

MALE

FEMALE

Lionesses average about two-thirds the size of male lions.

In a fight, who do you think would win? A lion or a tiger?

Male and female tigers look similar, but males are bigger. The males also have longer whiskers.

MALE   FEMALE

Tale of the Tape

MALE TIGER
AVERAGES
WEIGHT:
650 POUNDS
LENGTH:
10 FEET

Female tigers average about two-thirds the size of male tigers.

So look at the facts! Who do you think has an advantage? Who would win?

Lions have huge paws with long sharp claws. When walking, the claws do not touch the ground. But when provoked, the lion can extend its claws.

FUN FACT:
The claws are hidden by fur which is twice as long around the toes.

ACTUAL
SIZE
LION
CLAW

Lion's front left paw

Tigers also have huge paws. Tigers can leap fifteen feet high but can also quietly tiptoe like a ballerina. Lion and tiger footprints are called "pug marks."

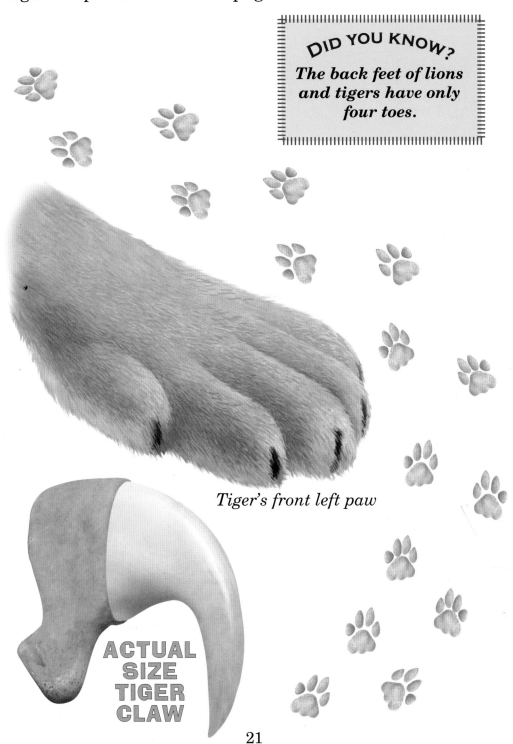

Tiger's front left paw

ACTUAL SIZE TIGER CLAW

Lions live in family groups called prides. A typical pride includes three males, fifteen lionesses, and two dozen cubs. Lions are unique—they are the only wild cats who live in a family.

DID YOU KNOW?

A big male lion leads his pride for about two years. He is often challenged by other big males. The challenge usually ends in a fight to the death.

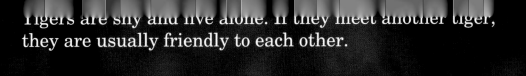

Tigers are shy and live alone. If they meet another tiger, they are usually friendly to each other.

Bonus Fact

Tigers might be found together when sharing a huge meal. A group of tigers is called a streak.

Baby lions are called cubs. Lion cubs are not plain brown. They are spotted. The spots help them to be camouflaged. As they grow up, they lose their spots.

DEFINITION

*The word **camouflaged** means able to hide or blend in with one's surroundings.*

DID YOU KNOW?

After a hunt, the male lion eats first, the lionesses eat next, and the cubs eat last.

Tiger cubs look like their parents. Tiger cubs are cute!

No, you cannot have one as a pet. When they grow up, they will eat you!

SPEED LIMIT 50

Lions have long tails and a clump of darker-colored fur on the end.

Tigers have long, striped tails.

SPEED
LIMIT
50

Bonus Fact

*A tiger's big tail
helps it balance
in a fight, or while
climbing trees.*

Bonus Fact

Lions, tigers, and jaguars are the only cats that roar.

The lion has a Siberian tiger in his sights. He **roars**—lions are loud! They can be heard five miles away, frightening every creature around.

The tiger sees the lion and roars back. Tigers are not as loud as lions, but now every animal in the area is alert.

FUN FACT:
Tigers purr in between roars. Their purr sounds like
"ooooooonnn"
as they exhale!

The tiger waits as the lion makes the first move. They wrestle, teeth and claws bared. Both cats are up on their hind legs.

The tiger tries to bite the lion in the neck. It does no good. Every time the tiger bites the lion in the neck, it is like biting a giant hairball. The lion's mane gives the lion a defensive advantage.

The fight is vicious. The big cats bite and claw at each other. First the quick lion, then the agile tiger, is on top. The fight goes back and forth. Each cat is a magnificent fighter.

The tiger gets the advantage and bites the lion's neck again. However, the lion's mane is like biting a giant mattress. The tiger is a better fighter, but he is getting tired of biting a fur ball. Eventually the lion grabs the tiger by the neck.

The lion's bite causes fatal damage. The tiger is defeated.

The lion limps away in victory. It has many cuts and bruises.

The lion won today. Nature has given lions a wonderful gift—a big thick fuzzy mane.

Will a tiger ever be able to beat a lion?

What would happen if a hammerhead shark came face-to-face with a bull shark? What if they were both the same size? What if they were both hungry? If they had a fight, who do you think would win?

GREAT HAMMERHEAD SHARK

Its head has a strange shape.

MAKO SHARK

The fastest-swimming shark!

REMEMBER THIS!
Fish have gills, not lungs.

MEGAMOUTH SHARK

A recently discovered deepwater shark with a huge mouth.

BULL SHARK

This shark has attacked more people
than any other shark.

WHALE SHARK

The largest fish in the world. It is a harmless filter feeder.

GREAT WHITE SHARK

The famous movie star
needs no introduction!

> **FACT**
> *Sharks are*
> *saltwater fish.*

TIGER SHARK

The "garbage can" of the sea.
It eats almost everything.

Meet the great hammerhead. It can grow to be twenty feet long and can weigh one thousand pounds. Hammerhead sharks are easy to identify, because they have a head shaped like a hammer.

FUN FACT
Scientists call the hammer-shaped head a cephalofoil.

DID YOU KNOW?
The largest hammerheads have a head that is three feet wide eyeball to eyeball.

Hammerheads look scary, but they hardly ever attack humans.

Meet the bull shark. It got its name from its stocky shape and unpredictable behavior. It is an aggressive shark that lives in shallow water, preferring water less than one hundred feet deep. Female bull sharks grow to be twelve feet long and to weigh five hundred pounds.

INTERESTING FACT
Great white sharks often get blamed for bull shark attacks.

DID YOU KNOW?
Because they live in shallow waters, bull sharks are more dangerous to people than great white sharks or tiger sharks, which prefer deep waters.

Hammerheads hunt by themselves at night. During the

Bull sharks prefer to be alone.

BONUS FACT
Despite their solitary nature, bull sharks sometimes hunt in twos.

SHARK TRIVIA
The bull shark has many names: Zambezi shark, estuary shark, java shark, Fitzroy Creek shark, ground shark, Swan River whaler, cub shark, freshwater shark, and Lake Nicaragua shark.

TYPES OF HAMMERHEADS

FUN FACT

The funny-shaped head allows them to have more sensors. Hammerheads can smell better and sense fish better than other sharks.

BONNETHEAD

GREAT

SCALLOPED

SMOOTH

DID YOU KNOW?

Some other hammerhead species are the scoophead, golden hammerhead, whitefin hammerhead, winghead shark, and scalloped bonnethead.

BULL SHARK
TRAVELS

Bull sharks swim in shallow coastal water. They often swim into estuaries and up freshwater rivers.

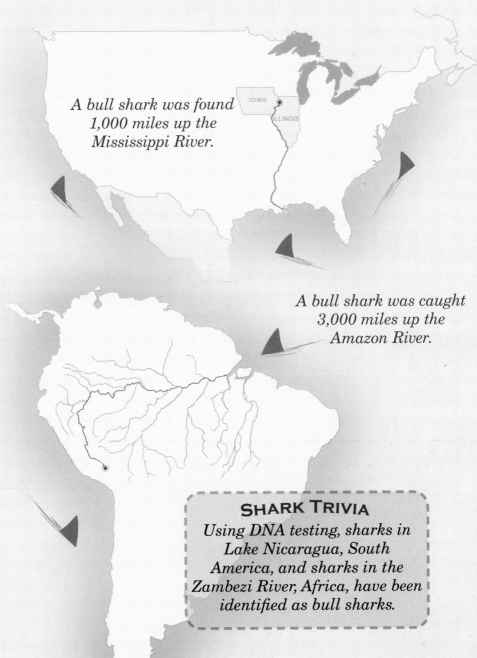

A bull shark was found 1,000 miles up the Mississippi River.

A bull shark was caught 3,000 miles up the Amazon River.

SHARK TRIVIA

Using DNA testing, sharks in Lake Nicaragua, South America, and sharks in the Zambezi River, Africa, have been identified as bull sharks.

If you were scuba diving and a hammerhead swam at you, this is what it would look like.

If you were skin diving and a bull shark swam right at you, this is what you would see. Yikes!

FUN FACT

Bull sharks' heads are wider than they are long.

DID YOU KNOW?

Bull sharks are known for bumping their prey first. After the bump, they decide if they want to bite.

HAMMERHEAD TOOTH

Compared to other sharks, hammerheads have small mouths. But hammerheads, like all sharks, have scary-looking teeth!

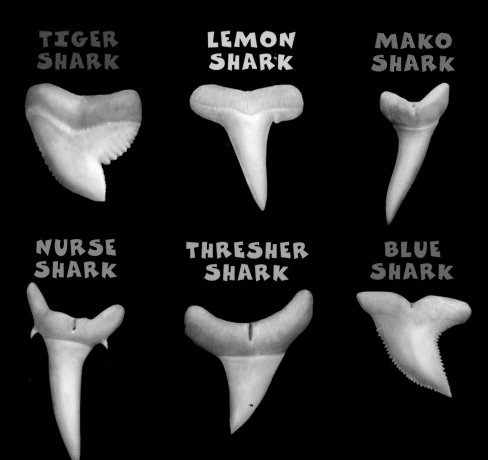

TIGER SHARK

LEMON SHARK

MAKO SHARK

NURSE SHARK

THRESHER SHARK

BLUE SHARK

BULL SHARK TOOTH

The bull shark has pointy bottom teeth and triangular top teeth. Its mouth is like a knife and fork. The bottom teeth hold the fish it catches, and the top jaw goes back and forth and cuts like a saw.

GREAT WHITE SHARK

GOBLIN SHARK

BLACKTIP SHARK

CROCODILE SHARK

WHALE SHARK

’

SAW SHARK

ANATOMY OF A HAMMERHEAD

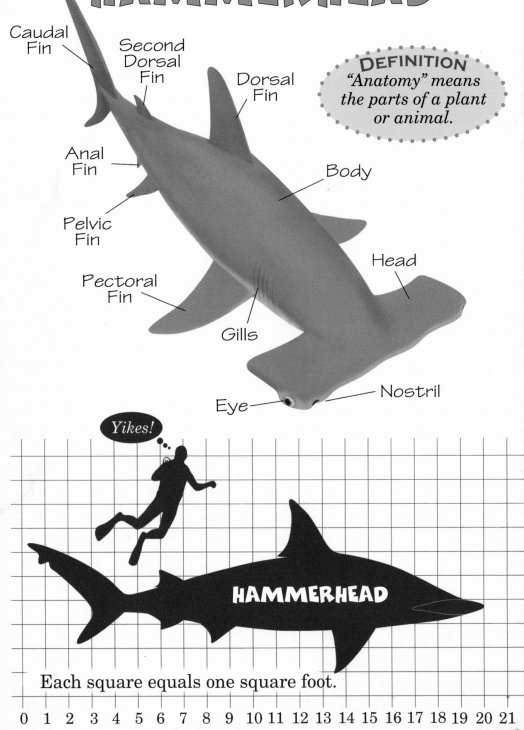

Caudal Fin

Second Dorsal Fin

Dorsal Fin

Anal Fin

Body

Pelvic Fin

Head

Pectoral Fin

Gills

Eye

Nostril

DEFINITION
"Anatomy" means the parts of a plant or animal.

Yikes!

HAMMERHEAD

Each square equals one square foot.

0 1 2 3 4 5 6 7 8 9 10 11 12 13 14 15 16 17 18 19 20 21

ANATOMY OF A BULL SHARK

Caudal
Fin

Second
Dorsal
Fin

Dorsal
Fin

Body

Anal
Fin

Pelvic
Fin

Head

Pectoral
Fin

Nostril

Eye

Gills

Oh, no!

BULL SHARK

Each square equals one square foot.

0 1 2 3 4 5 6 7 8 9 10 11 12 13

When engineers design aircraft, sometimes all they have to do is look at nature.

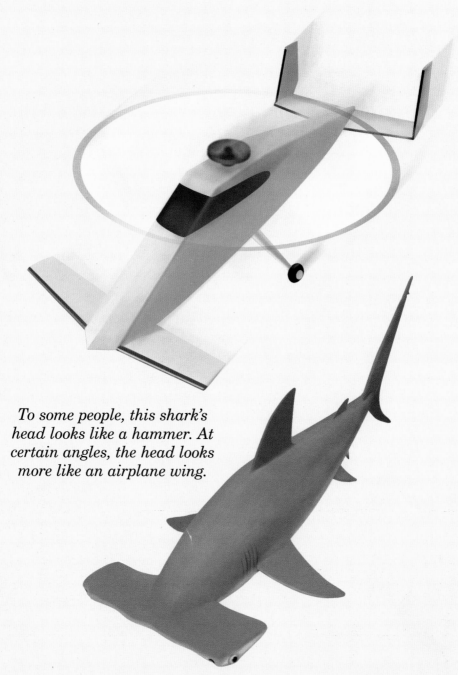

To some people, this shark's head looks like a hammer. At certain angles, the head looks more like an airplane wing.

The wing-shaped head gives the shark stability when it is swimming.

You could say that the space shuttle was designed by nature millions of years ago.

Look at the shape and design of the bull shark.

SHARK

The great hammerhead and the
bull shark are different sharks,
but their tails are similar.
Take a look!

**GREAT
HAMMERHEAD
SHARK**

**WHALE
SHARK**

**NURSE
SHARK**

**COOKIECUTTER
SHARK**

FUN FACT
*A ragged-tooth shark can
touch its tail with its nose.*

BONUS FACT
*A tail fin is also
called a caudal fin.*

TAILS

A shark uses its tail to propel itself forward. It steers with its tail and its side fins.

BULL SHARK

BONUS FACT
Almost all sharks have a vertical tail.

THRESHER SHARK

BLACKTIP REEF SHARK

TIGER SHARK

Sharks and pilot fish are friends.

For example, pilot fish eat parasites off the shark's skin. Pilot fish get to eat the shark's leftover food scraps. And pilot fish stay safe from predators by swimming with the shark.

TOUGH FACT
*Sharks have rough skin—
it is like armor. They have teeth on
their skin called denticles.*

DID YOU KNOW?
*Cleaner wrasses are fish that clean
sharks' skin. Some even go in the
sharks' mouths.*

SHARK HITCHHIKERS

Remoras are fish that hitch a ride on the shark. Remoras have a suction disc and attach themselves.

SHARK TRIVIA
Remoras are also called sharksuckers.

This is a remora.

ICKY FACT
Some parasitic copepods and worms attach themselves to sharks.

THINGS A HAMMERHEAD SHARK CAN'T DO

They can't parachute.

They can't sing like Elvis.

They can't ride a bicycle.

THINGS A BULL SHARK CAN'T DO

They can't yo-yo.

They can't paint
like Michelangelo.

They can't bake
cupcakes.

A giant hammerhead is cruising along. A bull shark is looking for food.

The hammerhead sees the bull shark, but is not interested. Huge sharks are not his type of food. The hammerhead looks for something smaller and easier to eat.

DID YOU KNOW?

The ferocious bull shark easily adapts to captivity and living in an aquarium.

The bull shark feels threatened and is not afraid to pick a fight. He swims right at the hammerhead.

The bull shark opens its mouth and tries to ram the hammerhead. The hammerhead's better eyesight allows him to turn and avoid the bull shark. The hammerhead dodges away.

The bull shark is angry and darts at the hammerhead again. The hammerhead ducks. Both sharks are excellent swimmers.

The bull shark attacks
again. This time it bites
the hammerhead's tail.
The hammerhead turns to
defend itself. But the bull
shark catches a piece of the
hammerhead's tail and
rips off a chunk.

The hammerhead is bleeding and can't swim as fast.
His blood excites the bull shark even more. At full speed,
the bull shark rams the hammerhead and knocks him
off balance. The bull shark bites the hammerhead a few
more times.

The hammerhead is defeated. The bull shark will eat him. Other sharks in the area can smell the meal.

The bull shark won today. Maybe the next time these two species meet, the hammerhead will recognize the danger right away.

WHO WOULD WIN?

POLAR BEAR VS. GRIZZLY BEAR

During the Arctic winter, polar bears and grizzly bears live far away from each other. But during the summer months, while looking for food, polar bears and grizzly bears sometimes end up in the same location.

What would happen if they met each other? What would happen if they had a fight? Who would win?

SCIENTIFIC NAME OF POLAR BEAR
"Ursus maritimus"

Meet the polar bear. Polar bears are considered sea mammals. They spend most of their time on the frozen sea. They prefer to live near the edge of the ice pack. They are the largest of all bears.

FUN FACT

There are no polar bears in Antarctica.

REMEMBER

Polar bears: North Pole.
Penguins: South Pole.
There are no penguins in the Arctic.

SCIENTIFIC NAME OF GRIZZLY BEAR
"Ursus arctos horribilis"

Meet the grizzly bear. Grizzly bears are mammals that live on land. You can tell grizzlies by the huge hump at their shoulders. This is a muscle they use for digging.

DID YOU KNOW?
There are no grizzly bears in the southern hemisphere.

Sorry, black bear. You are not in this book because you are not as big and ferocious as grizzlies and polar bears.

Forget about it, giant panda. You are a plant eater and are no match for a polar bear or a grizzly.

Polar bears have snow-white fur. Their color allows them to blend in with their environment—snow, slush, and ice.

WHITE FUR

POLAR BEAR NAMES

Ice bear, nanook, white bear, sea bear

DID YOU KNOW?

A polar bear's white fur is actually translucent. Translucent means see-through or clear.

Grizzly bears come in four different colors: dark brown, brown, reddish brown, and blond.

DARK
BROWN

BROWN

REDDISH
BROWN

BLOND

These colors allow grizzlies to blend in with their environment—fallen leaves, dirt, rocks, and trees.

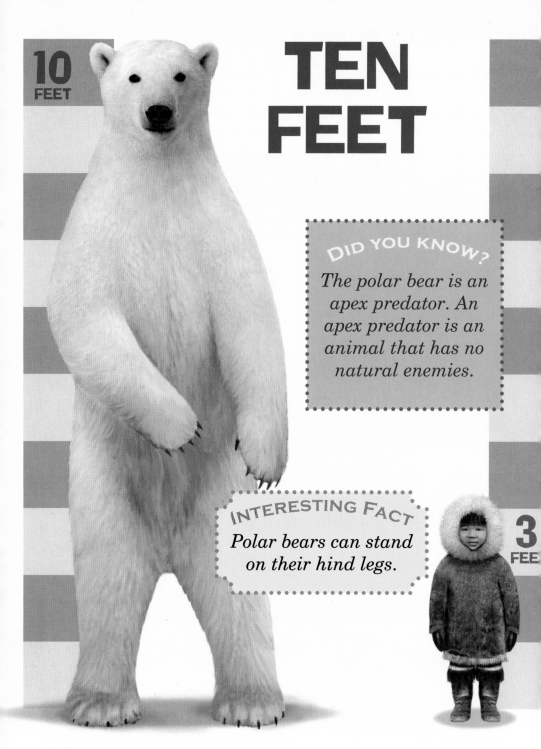

TEN FEET

DID YOU KNOW?

The polar bear is an apex predator. An apex predator is an animal that has no natural enemies.

INTERESTING FACT

Polar bears can stand on their hind legs.

3
FEE

Polar bears are the largest predatory land animals. Polar bears can grow to be ten feet tall. Here is a kindergartner next to a polar bear.

EIGHT FEET

8 FEET

5 FEET

FUN FACT

Grizzlies can also stand on their hind legs.

A grizzly bear can stand eight feet tall. They tower over you.

A polar bear paw is larger than this book.

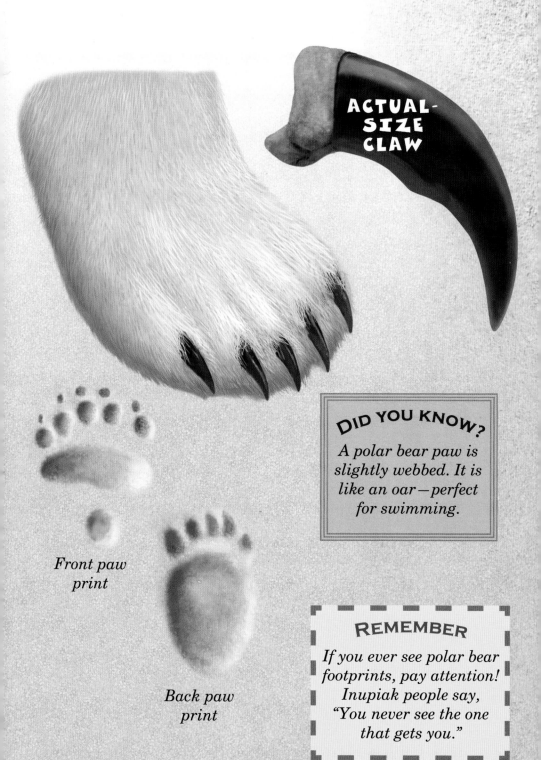

ACTUAL-SIZE CLAW

Front paw print

Back paw print

DID YOU KNOW?

A polar bear paw is slightly webbed. It is like an oar—perfect for swimming.

REMEMBER

If you ever see polar bear footprints, pay attention! Inupiak people say, "You never see the one that gets you."

74

This is a grizzly track. A track is a footprint.
Their front claws can be four inches long.

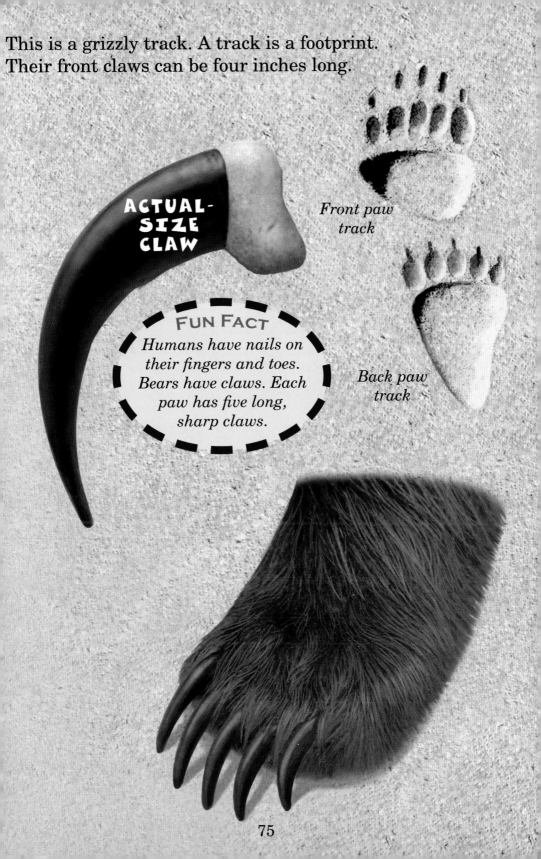

ACTUAL-
SIZE
CLAW

Front paw
track

Back paw
track

FUN FACT

*Humans have nails on
their fingers and toes.
Bears have claws. Each
paw has five long,
sharp claws.*

Polar bears are excellent swimmers. They can swim farther than fifty miles at one stretch.

Polar bears mostly eat meat from the ocean—walrus, seals, sea lions, and fish. Seals are their favorite food.

FUN FACT

Polar bears do the dog paddle.

DID YOU KNOW?

YIKES! A polar bear can eat a human, but it hardly ever happens. Not many people live near polar bears.

Grizzly bears are good swimmers, but they prefer standing in a river to catch fish. If a grizzly stands in the right spot, a migrating salmon might jump right into its mouth.

INTERESTING FACT

Grizzlies eat salmon, trout, apples, berries, honey, and anything they can get their paws on. Grizzlies have also been known to eat moose, elk, caribou, rodents, sheep, grubs, and clams.

NOT A FUN FACT

Each year grizzlies eat a few people.

Open wide! Polar bears have carnivore teeth—canine teeth in front and huge molars in back.

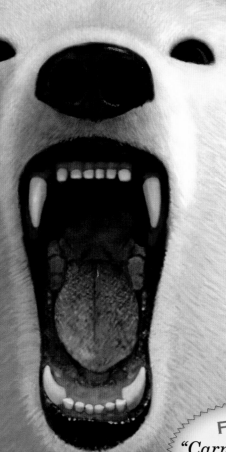

IMPORTANT FACT
Polar bears can smell a seal through ice three feet thick.

FUN FACT
"Carnivore" means "meat eater."

Grizzly bears have teeth that are similar to a polar bear's.

Grizzlies have such a good sense of smell that they can detect a dead animal ten miles away.

A polar bear can run twenty-five miles per hour. That is faster than a human can run. Polar bears can run down some caribou!

So who would win if they had a fight? The polar bear or the grizzly bear?

Grizzly bears look slow. But don't be fooled. Grizzly bears can easily outrun a human. They are fast!

DID YOU KNOW?
A grizzly is faster on land. A polar bear is probably faster on ice.

Here is a polar bear skeleton.

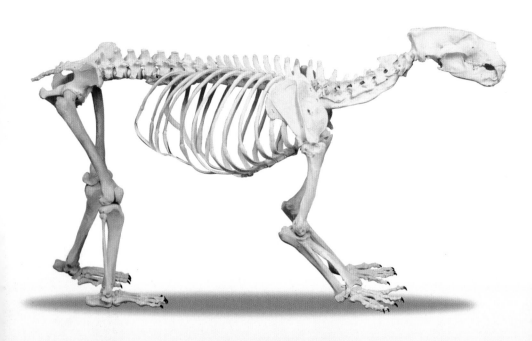

GOOFY FACT
*All polar bears are
left-handed.*

INTERESTING FACT

*The sun bear from Asia grows to be
only about five feet tall, the average
height of a human.*

Bear skeletons are somewhat similar to a human's.
Four limbs, five fingers, five toes, backbone, ribs, head,
neck, and hips.

Here is the complete skeleton of a grizzly bear.

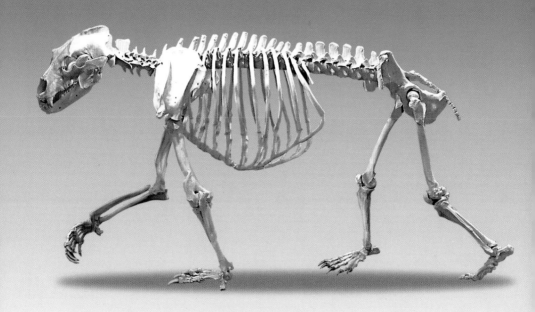

SAD FACT
The silver bear from Mexico was hunted to extinction.

INTERESTING FACT

Scientists have studied bear DNA and think that the polar bear and the grizzly bear are descended from the same animal. Both adapted to their environments. Polar bears prefer the sea. Grizzlies prefer to live on land. Only an expert osteologist, a bone scientist, can tell their bones apart.

Polar bears are solitary animals. They rarely fight each other, and mostly they stay away from each other.

Grizzly bears are also solitary animals. But groups of grizzlies sometimes fish together during a salmon migration.

Male polar bears do not hibernate. They spend all winter looking for food. They might build a snow cave to sleep away an unusually bad storm.

SNOW CAVE

Female polar bears build a "maternity den," usually in the snow and ice, to spend the winter and take care of their cubs. This conserves the mom's energy.

DID YOU KNOW?

Hibernation is when an animal goes into a resting state of inactivity, with a slower heartbeat, no eating or drinking, and a lower body temperature.

ROCK CAVE

Just before winter, grizzlies eat as much as they can
to fatten up for a long sleep. Grizzly bears have a deep
winter sleep, but it is not true hibernation. A grizzly can
wake up and suddenly attack you. In the springtime,
grizzlies are hungry. Watch out!

FUNNY POLAR BEAR STORIES

A US Navy nuclear sub surfaced in the Arctic ice, only to find a few polar bears snooping around.

Sometimes polar bears take naps in the funniest of positions.

A famous nature photographer waited for days to get a good picture of a polar bear. He was eating lunch in his pickup truck one day when he saw a big surprise in his rearview mirror.

FUNNY GRIZZLY BEAR STORIES

An Alaskan man came home to find a grizzly bear relaxing in his jacuzzi.

A sailor anchored in a harbor in Alaska was awakened by a noise. He found a grizzly walking around his yacht. Scared out of his wits, he pushed the grizzly off with an oar.

Using a cheeseburger, a tourist lured a grizzly bear into his car. The foolish man wanted to get a nice picture of the bear sitting with his wife. The woman screamed, and the confused bear ran away.

It is summer.

A polar bear steps off the ice onto a beach. A grizzly bear comes out of the woods.

They see each other. They can smell each other. Both bears stand to get a better look. Then it happens. The grizzly charges at the polar bear, growling and showing his teeth.

The polar bear crouches down, paws up, ready for battle. Running at full speed, the grizzly knocks over the polar bear.

The polar bear gets right up and fights back. Whap! He smacks the grizzly in the face. Ouch! They claw, scratch, and bite. It's a nasty fight.

They wrestle, each trying to get the advantage.

Rolling around, both bears get dirty from the sand and mud.

The grizzly is relentless—it keeps on fighting!

Suddenly, the polar bear sees no point in fighting anymore. There is no reason to fight to the death. The polar bear runs away.

The grizzly wins. But now he is sore and tired. He hopes he never runs into a polar bear again. These two bears are so similar—next time the outcome could be quite different!

WHO WOULD WIN?

HORNET VS. WASP

What would happen if a hornet came face-to-face with a wasp? What if they had a fight? Who do you think would win? Learn facts. Make a prediction!

MEET A HORNET

I am an Asian giant hornet. My scientific name is *Vespa mandarinia*. There are about 2,000 different types of hornets. I am one of the largest and most aggressive hornets—I sting multiple times.

ACTUAL SIZE

AMAZING

The Asian giant hornet is the largest in the world.

Don't call me a bee. I'm not a bee, and I don't make honey. I am a hornet!

MEET A WASP

I am a wasp. I am slightly orange and have a skinny waist. I am a paper wasp, and my scientific name is *Polistes perplexus*. Don't come near me, or I might sting you.

ACTUAL SIZE

Don't even think about calling me a bee. I am a wasp!

INSECTS

Ants, bees, hornets, and wasps are similar. Scientists say they are related. Their bodies have three parts:

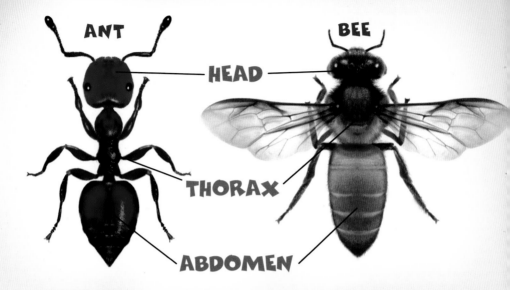

ANT

BEE

HEAD

THORAX

ABDOMEN

LEG FACT
Insects have six legs. The legs are attached to the thorax.

FLYING FACT
Bees, hornets, and wasps have wings. Most ants do not.

HORNET

WASP

Look at their bodies. All four insects have a similar body type.

COMPARE

A spider body has two parts—cephalothorax and abdomen.

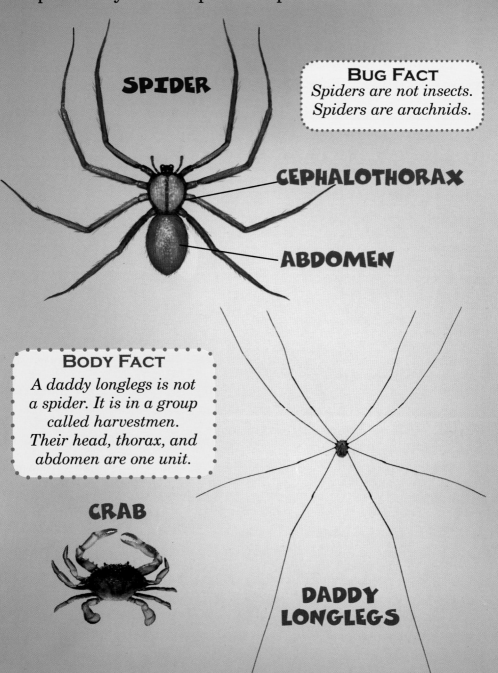

SPIDER

BUG FACT
Spiders are not insects.
Spiders are arachnids.

CEPHALOTHORAX

ABDOMEN

BODY FACT

A daddy longlegs is not a spider. It is in a group called harvestmen. Their head, thorax, and abdomen are one unit.

CRAB

DADDY LONGLEGS

A crab also has its head, thorax, and abdomen as one unit.

BEES

Bees pollinate plants. These insects pick up pollen (a special powder) on their legs and bring it to another plant, which helps the plants reproduce.

GREEN BEE

HONEYBEE

STRANGE FACT
Honeybee front legs are for walking and for cleaning their antennae.

FUN FACT
Bee legs are for collecting pollen.

BUMBLEBEE

CARPENTER BEE

FUZZY FACT
Most bees are hairy and fuzzy.

MORE ABOUT BEES

There are about 20,000 different species of bees. They live everywhere in the world where there are flowers. Bees do not live in Antarctica.

COLLETID BEE

LEAFCUTTER BEE

COOL FACT
Honey is bee throw-up.

CUCKOO BEE

ORCHID BEE

COLOR FACT
Bees come in many colors.

FLOWERS

Trees, bushes, flowers, weeds, vegetables, and other plants all have flowers. The honeybee visits them all.

rose
flower

apple
blossom

STAMEN

STIGMA

forsythia
flower

PETAL

OVULE

knapweed
flower

corn
flower

DID YOU KNOW?
Worker bees collect nectar from flowers. They have a brush on the end of their tongues.

HONEY

Honey is sweet food that bees make for their hive. The honey is made when honeybees collect nectar from flowers and partially digest it. They then fly back to the hive and regurgitate it into the honeycomb.

DEFINITION

Regurgitate *means to throw up.*

FACT

One honeybee makes $\frac{1}{12}$ of a teaspoon of honey in its life.

There are three types of bees in the honeybee hive: one queen bee, drones, and worker bees.

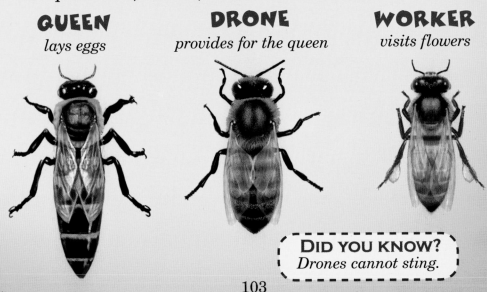

QUEEN
lays eggs

DRONE
provides for the queen

WORKER
visits flowers

DID YOU KNOW?
Drones cannot sting.

WHAT A FACE

How do you like my hornet face? I am so awesome, I should be making science-fiction movies in Hollywood. I could be a star!

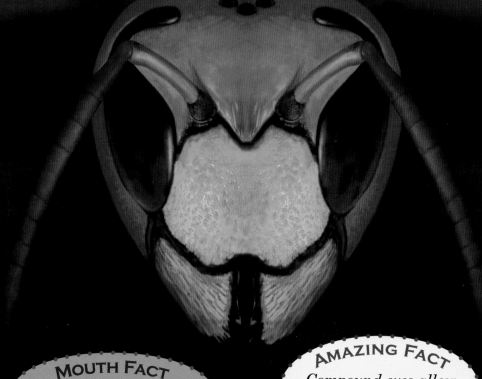

DID YOU KNOW?
Hornets, wasps, and bees have compound eyes.

MOUTH FACT
Hornets have strong jaws. They bite!

AMAZING FACT
Compound eyes allow insects to see multiple images at once.

I am very aggressive. You could say that I have a bad

ANOTHER GREAT FACE

How do you like my wasp face? I am so good-looking, I should be a Halloween mask. I could scare you!

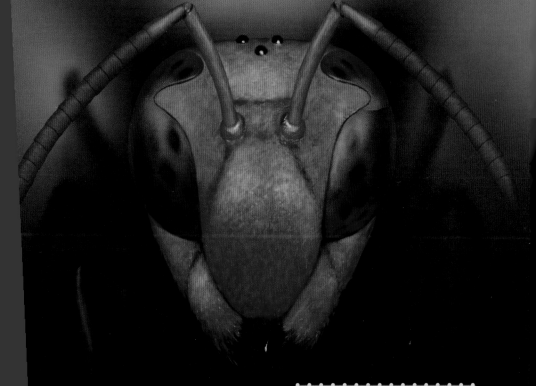

FACT
Wasps and hornets have compound eyes, but they also have three small eyes on the top of their heads.

BITE FACT
Wasps have strong jaws, too!

DID YOU KNOW?
Wasps and hornets can feel, taste, and hear with their antennae.

If you bother me, I also can be nasty.

HORNET HOMES

This is where I live—a hornet's nest.

PAPER NEST

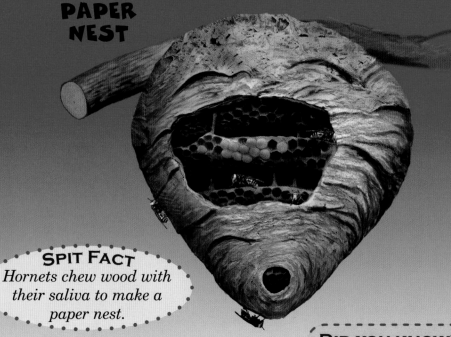

DID YOU KNOW?
The interior of a large hornet's nest has different levels to house larvae.

UMBRELLA NEST

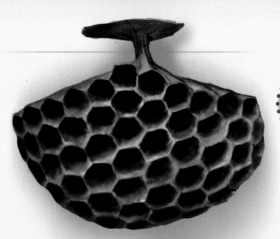

DEFINITION
A larva is a newly hatched insect that resembles a worm.

FUN FACT
Hornets made paper before humans.

WASP HOMES

I am a wasp, and I prefer to live underground.

UNDERGROUND NEST

FACT
Wasps dig their own tunnels or sometimes find an abandoned burrow.

UNDERGROUND PAPER NEST CROSS SECTION

Sometimes I build a mud nest. I might even build it in your house.

MUD NEST CUTAWAY

MUD FACT
Wasps mix dirt and spit to make mud.

MUD NEST

DIET

Do you wonder what I eat? I am a hornet; I don't care for nectar or those goofy flowers. I like to eat other bugs.

I sometimes eat dead animals, or maybe your garbage.

DIET

I am a wasp. I eat meat—mostly spiders, caterpillars, bugs, and other insects. I like to eat human food, too.

FUN FACT
On a picnic, a wasp may go after your cheeseburger.

DID YOU KNOW?
A wasp would visit a flower and drink a little nectar.

TOO NASTY ! TO SHOW

Wasps like roadkill. It is common for people to find a dead snake covered with hungry wasps.

WINGS AND LEGS

Hornets have four wings. Each side of the hornet has a fore wing and a hind wing. They hook together while in flight.

FORE WING

HIND WING

FUN FACT
A hornet's leg has multiple joints. Each leg has more than one knee.

Close-up of hamuli

I don't like wasps, except for dinner!

THAT'S AMAZING!
A hornet can flap its wings about 10,000 times per minute.

LEGS AND WINGS

Wasps also have four wings.

FACT
Insects do not have bones. They have an outer shell called an exoskeleton.

WING FACT
Hornet and wasp wings are made of the same material as their exoskeleton.

Hey, buddy, I'm going to eat you soon!

HORNET STINGER

A honeybee will sting you once and then die. A hornet can sting over and over again.

FACT
The abdomen of the hornet is segmented. It can swivel around and line up a perfect sting.

This is a close-up of a hornet stinger. It has tiny ridges.

DEFINITION
Segmented *means made of different sections.*

CAN YOU?
Can you outrun a hornet? Hornets fly about 15 miles per hour.

WASP STINGER

A wasp has a smooth stinger. A wasp can also sting multiple times!

OTHER ANIMALS THAT STING
Bees, stingrays, jellyfish, platypuses, and scorpions.

This is a close-up of a wasp stinger.

SPEED FACTS
An Olympic sprinter runs 26 miles per hour. A wasp can fly up to 17 miles per hour. A third grader can run up to 12 miles per hour.

FACT
The wasp's and hornet's abdomen can swivel 360 degrees.

Just looking at the stingers can make you shiver.

HISTORY

Hornets have been on earth for more than 150 million years. Hornets and dinosaurs once lived together.

HELP! MOM!

QUESTION?
How many hornets would it take to aggravate a T. rex?

Here is a hornet trapped in amber.

DEFINITION
Amber is hardened tree resin.

DID YOU KNOW?
An insect can be preserved in amber for millions of years.

HISTORY

FACT
Wasps also lived millions of years ago.

Would this be a good WHO WOULD WIN? book?
APATOSAURUS VS. WASP

DEFINITION
A fossil is the impression of a prehistoric plant or animal preserved in rock.

Look at this 125-million-year-old fossil. The wasp hasn't changed much. Look at the segmented body, wings, and antennae.

OTHER HORNETS

This is a fighter jet. It is called the F/A-18 Hornet. Like a hornet, it can "sting" multiple times.

AIR SHOW FACT
The Blue Angels fly F/A-18s.

F/A-18 HORNETS

The Blue Angels are the U.S. Navy's flight-demonstration team.

NAME FACT
The Sacramento State University sports teams call themselves the Hornets.

HORNETS
SACRAMENTO STATE

AN HONOR

There is a U.S. Navy LHD-1 ship called the USS *Wasp*. It is an assault ship.

DID YOU KNOW?
LHD *stands for* "Landing Helicopter Dock."

FACT
Eight U.S. Navy ships have been named Wasp.

DID YOU KNOW?
There is a rugby team in England called the London Wasps.

LONDON
WASPS
®

The "wasp waist" style was fashionable in the eighteenth and nineteenth centuries.

TRUE HORNET STORY

When he was a boy, the illustrator of this book was stung by a swarm of hornets after stepping on a nest by mistake.

HORNET JEWELRY

Some people make hornet jewelry.

DEFINITION
A brooch is an ornament or jewelry that has a pin on the back.

brooch

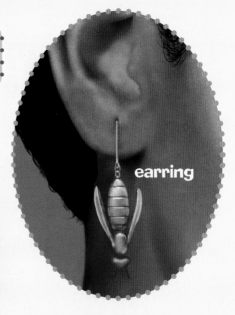

earring

118

TRUE WASP STORY

When the author of this book was in Little League, he was stung by a wasp while at bat.

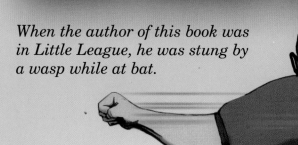

The umpire thought the batter was complaining about the called third strike.

WASP JEWELRY

Would you wear a wasp ring?

DEFINITION

A necklace is jewelry worn around the neck.

ring

necklace

The hornet is flying near a dragonfly. It doesn't see the wasp flying nearby.

With no warning, the hornet attacks, but the wasp stings the hornet in the eye.

The wounded hornet flies in circles to figure out what happened. The wasp decides to fly away and avoid a battle.

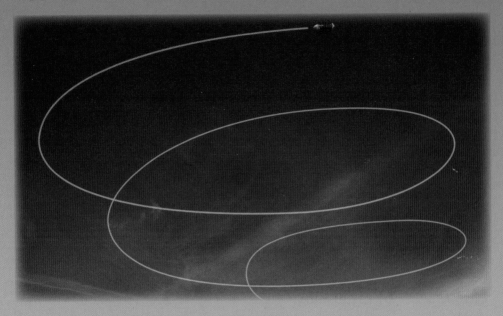

The hornet darts after the wasp. It attacks and stings the wasp several times.

The wasp drops to the ground to try to escape. The hornet stings hurt! The hornet follows.

It stings the wasp two more times in the head. The wasp tries to fight back, but it can't. It is severely wounded.

The wasp dies of its wounds. The hornet's eye is injured, but the fight is over. The hornet has won.

It decides to eat the wasp.

WHO WOULD WIN?

TRICERATOPS VS. SPINOSAURUS

Author note:
Triceratops and Spinosaurus lived on different
continents, millions of years apart. But what
might have happened if they met?

Millions and millions of years ago, dinosaurs walked on Earth. What would have happened if a Triceratops met a Spinosaurus? Would they have had a fight? If they had, who do you think would win?

MEET TRICERATOPS

This dinosaur's name means "three-horned face." It was a herbivore that walked on four legs. Its mouth was shaped like a beak.

DEFINITION
A herbivore is an animal that eats only plants.

FACT
Today's alligators and crocodiles have legs that come out of the sides of their bodies.

DID YOU KNOW?
All dinosaurs had legs directly under their bodies.

Triceratops did not have an exceptionally long tail. It looked evenly balanced on all four legs.

MEET
SPINOSAURUS

Spinosaurus means "spine lizard." It had a long backbone made up of many vertebrae, or bony parts. The tall spines on its back formed a sail. Spinosaurus was a carnivore.

CARNIVORE
A carnivore is an animal that eats meat.

SIZE FACT
Spinosaurus was the largest meat-eating dinosaur. Sorry, Tyrannosaurus rex, you were smaller.

Spinosaurus lived in swamps and was probably a great swimmer. Its mouth was perfectly shaped for catching fish.

PALEONTOLOGY

Paleontology is the study of the past by digging for and learning about fossils. How do we know dinosaurs lived on Earth? While digging, people have discovered fossilized bones that are larger and different from those of animals that currently live on Earth.

This is a dinosaur fossil that was discovered by paleontologists during a dinosaur dig. Sometimes only fragments are found, and it's difficult to identify the dinosaur.

FACT
A fossil is bone, teeth, or other matter preserved by rocks and minerals for thousands or millions of years.

DEFINITION
A paleontologist is a scientist who studies the past through fossils and rock formations.

ARCHAEOLOGY

Archaeologists dig, dig, and dig to find ancient buried buildings and cities. Sometimes while excavating a site, archaeologists discover fossilized bones of extinct creatures.

Where would you rather work? On a dinosaur dig or an ancient-city dig? If you discovered a new dinosaur, what would you call it?

DEFINITION

Archaeology scientifically studies ancient peoples and cultures by excavating sites.

ELECTRONIC TOOLS

Modern tools such as satellites and sonar are used to hunt and find dinosaur fossils.

SATELLITE

A satellite beaming a signal to Earth.

SONAR

A scientist with equipment beaming sound waves at a fossil underground.

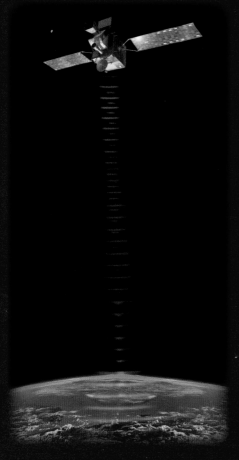

Electronic pulses and sound waves find unusual sites to start digging.

> **FACT**
> *Satellites and sonar are also used to find oil and natural gas.*

STANDARD TOOLS

There is no easy way to do a tough job. Eventually, paleontologists and archaeologists have to get their hands and clothes dirty. They dig with picks, trowels, and shovels.

PICKS　　**DIGGERS**　　**BRUSHES**

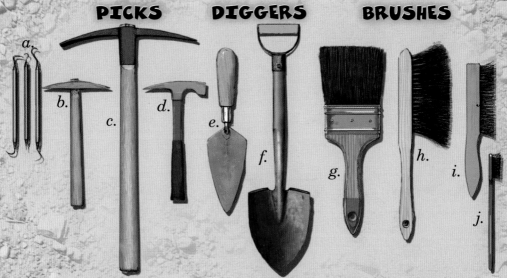

Small details are important. Big tools are eventually put aside, and brushes, magnifying glasses, and tiny tools are carefully used to preserve important information.

OPTICAL

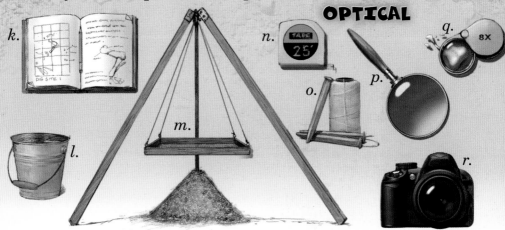

a. Dentist tools　　*g. Paint brush*　　*m. Sifting table*
b. Rock pick　　*h. Dust brush*　　*n. Measuring tape*
c. Pick mattock　　*i. Wire brush*　　*o. String, stakes*
d. Pick hammer　　*j. Toothbrush*　　*p. Magnifying glass*
e. Masonry trowel　　*k. Journal*　　*q. Jeweler's loupe*
f. Shovel　　*l. Bucket*　　*r. Camera*

BIG

How big was Triceratops? *Big!* Bigger than most elephants! Triceratops was roughly 30 feet long and 10 feet high and weighed up to 12 tons.

TRICERATOPS

TRI FACT
Triceratops was bigger than an African elephant, the heaviest land animal on Earth today.

WEIGHT CONVERSION
12 tons is equal to 24,000 pounds.

TEACHER

ELEPHANT

DID YOU KNOW?
The first dinosaur ever named was Megalosaurus.

HUGE

How huge was Spinosaurus? *Huge!* It was taller than a giraffe and longer than a humpback whale. It was about 60 feet long and weighed up to 9 tons.

SPINOSAURUS

KINDERGARTNER

GIRAFFE

FUN FACT
Not all dinosaurs were huge. Some grown-up dinosaurs, such as Compsognathus, were smaller than kindergartners.

DINOSAUR

In the late 1800s, two of the most famous dinosaur hunters were busy looking for fossils. They were friends at first and then bitter rivals: Othniel Charles Marsh and Edward Drinker Cope.

They discovered well over 100 new species of dinosaurs. Books and movies have been written about these scientists.

HUNTERS

Marsh worked to find fossils for the Peabody Museum of Natural History at Yale University. Cope hunted fossils for the Academy of Natural Sciences in Philadelphia. Here are some of the species they found:

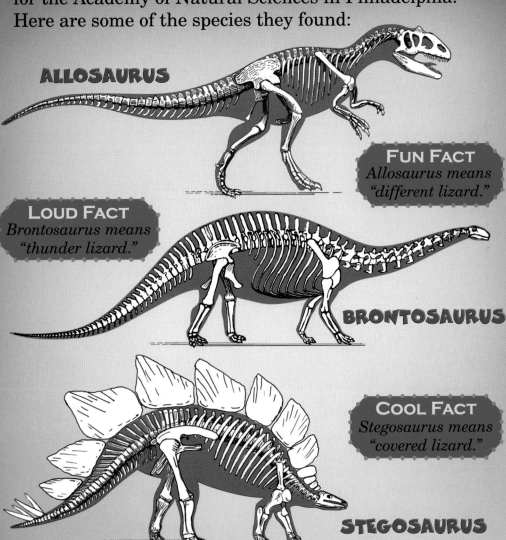

ALLOSAURUS

FUN FACT
Allosaurus means "different lizard."

LOUD FACT
Brontosaurus means "thunder lizard."

BRONTOSAURUS

COOL FACT
Stegosaurus means "covered lizard."

STEGOSAURUS

Most of the fossilized bones they discovered were in the American West, including Wyoming, Colorado, and Utah.

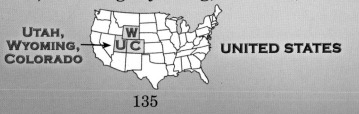

UTAH, WYOMING, COLORADO → **UNITED STATES**

TRICERATOPS SKELETON

This is a Triceratops skeleton. It was discovered in North America.

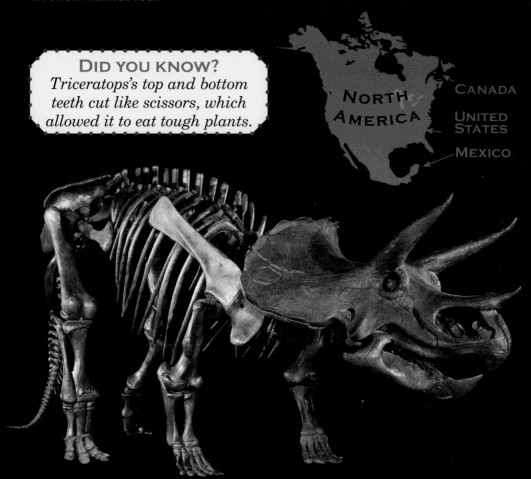

DID YOU KNOW?
Triceratops's top and bottom teeth cut like scissors, which allowed it to eat tough plants.

CANADA

NORTH AMERICA

UNITED STATES

MEXICO

Take a close look at the skeleton. Think of your own skeleton. What do you have in common with Triceratops? Its width, hands, tail, or beak? No. Four limbs, vertebrae, and ribs? Yes! Can you think of more?

FUN FACT
Dinosaurs are not the only extinct animals.

SPINOSAURUS SKELETON

This is a Spinosaurus skeleton. It was discovered in Morocco, on the continent of Africa.

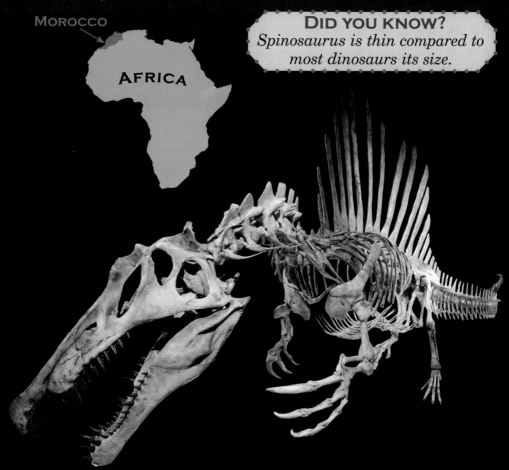

MOROCCO

AFRICA

DID YOU KNOW?
Spinosaurus is thin compared to most dinosaurs its size.

Notice how skinny Spinosaurus is. Is it shaped like a fish? Take a close look. What do you have in common with this skeleton? Its sail, three fingers, or long skinny jaw? No. Its two legs and ribs? Yes! Toenails? Maybe! What else? Think!

DINO FACT
Spinosaurus was not discovered until 1912.

FUN FACT
Not all animals have skeletons!

CERATOPSIANS

Ceratopsia means "horned face." Triceratops is a member of a group of dinosaurs called ceratopsians.

FACT
Torosaurus had one of the largest skulls of any land animal that ever lived on Earth.

PSITTACOSAURUS

TOROSAURUS

LEPTOCERATOPS

STYRACOSAURUS

FUN FACT
These other dinosaurs are also ceratopsians.

PENTACERATOPS

THEROPODS

Spinosaurs are in a group called theropods. Other theropods include Giganotosaurus, Tyrannosaurus rex, and Velociraptor.

DEFINITION
The word theropod means "beast foot."

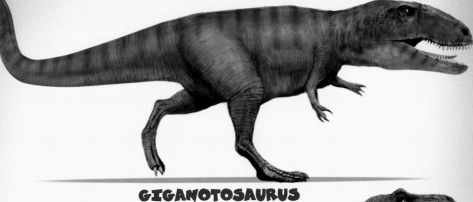

GIGANOTOSAURUS

TYRANNOSAURUS
REX

SALTOPUS

FACT
Most theropods were carnivores.

VELOCIRAPTOR

GALLIMIMUS

139

WHAT COLOR?

Nobody today really knows what color the dinosaurs were all those millions of years ago.

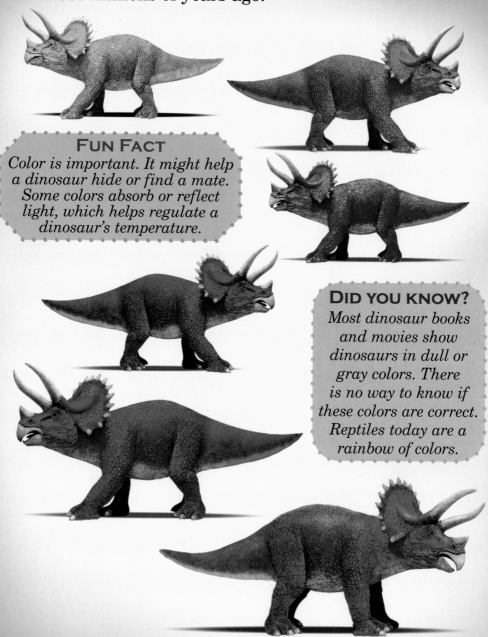

FUN FACT
Color is important. It might help a dinosaur hide or find a mate. Some colors absorb or reflect light, which helps regulate a dinosaur's temperature.

DID YOU KNOW?
Most dinosaur books and movies show dinosaurs in dull or gray colors. There is no way to know if these colors are correct. Reptiles today are a rainbow of colors.

What color do you think Triceratops was? In the animal kingdom, males are often a different color than females.

WHAT DESIGN?

And there's little proof of what skin patterns the dinosaurs may have had.

ZEBRA FACTS

Today there are zebras, zebrafish, zebra grass, zebra mussels, zebra finches, zebra longwing butterflies, and zebra sharks. Could Spinosaurus have had zebra stripes, too?

MOO

Maybe Spinosaurus was patterned like a cow.

PLEASE DO THIS

Someone, please get in a time machine and come back and tell us what color the dinosaurs were.

Think of the diversity of species and colors of animals living today. The color of Spinosaurus could have been any pattern or multiple designs.

WHERE, OH WHERE?

In 1923 in Mongolia, a clutch of fossilized dinosaur eggs were discovered. But no infants or toddlers were ever found.

EGG FACT
In France in 1859, a paleontologist discovered huge fossilized eggs. He thought they were giant bird eggs. We now know they were dinosaur eggs.

It puzzled the scientific community. Where were the babies? Where were the juveniles? It was a mystery.

MEET JACK HORNER

When Jack Horner was six years old, he found his first dinosaur bone.

As an adult, Jack served as a consultant on the Jurassic Park movies.

He may be the greatest dinosaur hunter who ever lived.

WHERE ARE THE BABIES?

In 1978, Jack Horner theorized that if adult dinosaurs and predators lived along the ocean coastline, the mothers and babies must have been in the foothills.

Jack dug in the foothills of Montana. This used to be the seacoast 150 million years ago. It took a while, but he was right. The baby jawbone he examined led the way to finding a Maiasaura nursery. The fossils proved that Maiasaura took care of its young.

JUVENILE JAWBONE

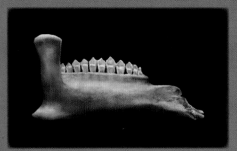

MAIASAURA EMBRYO

Jack was also the first to discover a dinosaur embryo.

SPEED

Triceratops looks slow. But it might have been a fast runner. A rhinoceros can run 30 miles per hour. Maybe Triceratops could do half that speed.

FOOTPRINTS

How do we know about dinosaur footprints? Dinosaurs walked in mud or clay, and then the mud dried and after many years became rock. Their footprints were preserved.

DID YOU KNOW?
A dinosaur footprint is a trace fossil. A trace fossil is an impression left behind by a dinosaur or other living thing.

QUICKNESS

The fastest living animal on two legs is an ostrich, which can run 45 miles per hour. Spinosaurus probably ran only about 15–20 miles per hour.

FOOTPRINTS

What did we learn when dinosaur footprints were discovered? There was no line between their feet. This meant they did not drag their tails along the ground.

FUN FACT
If you go to a national park and see dinosaur footprints, you are walking where dinosaurs once roamed.

DEFENSIVE ARMOR

Triceratops could be best described as a horned plant-eater.

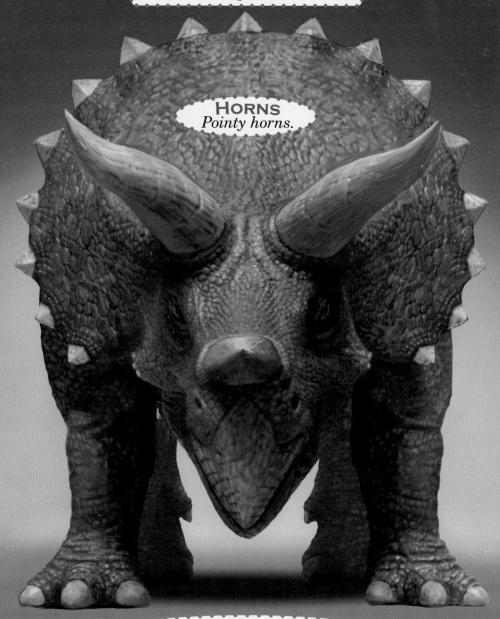

SHIELD
Its head has a protective shield.

HORNS
Pointy horns.

FOUR LEGS
Being steady on four legs and well balanced is a weapon in Triceratops's arsenal.

OFFENSIVE WEAPONS

Spinosaurus has great weapons.

BITE
Long jaw with sharp pointy teeth.

SHRED
Long fingers with sharp claws.

SMACK
Long tail to smack or swim with (scientists still aren't sure).

Triceratops is busy eating green leaves. Spinosaurus is roaming around looking for food. The two dinosaurs see each other. Triceratops walks away.

Hungry Spinosaurus jogs over to attack. Triceratops
runs away. This plant-eater does not want to fight.

Spinosaurus easily catches up and bites Triceratops.

Triceratops turns and faces Spinosaurus. The two
dinosaurs push each other back and forth.

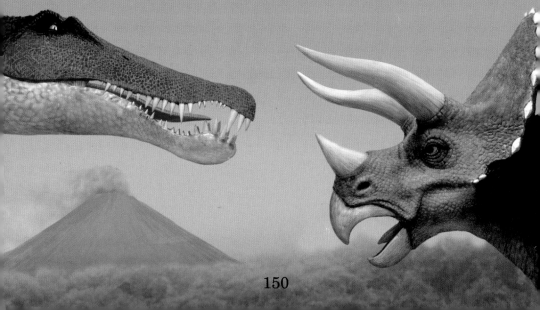

Triceratops charges Spinosaurus. They fight ferociously.

It is agility versus bony head frills; teeth and claws versus horns.

Nearby, a volcano erupts. Oh no! It's so smoky that no one can see what's happening. Ash is falling.

Ash and lava bury the two dinosaurs. But what happened?

It's one hundred million years later. We are on a dinosaur dig. The paleontologists have unearthed dinosaur fossils. Who won the fight? Turn the page for the answer.

WHO HAS THE ADVANTAGE?
CHECKLIST

LION		TIGER
☐	Fur	☐
☐	Teeth	☐
☐	Intelligence	☐
☐	Size	☐
☐	Hunting Skill	☐
☐	Claws	☐
☐	Hearing	☐
☐	Family	☐
☐	Speed	☐

Author note: This was one way the fight might have ended.
How would you write the ending?

WHO HAS THE ADVANTAGE?
CHECKLIST

HAMMERHEAD SHARK

BULL SHARK

HAMMERHEAD SHARK		BULL SHARK
☐	Length	☐
☐	Weight	☐
☐	Teeth	☐
☐	Vision	☐
☐	Head shape	☐

Author note: This is one way the fight might have ended. How would you write the ending?

WHO HAS THE ADVANTAGE?

CHECKLIST

POLAR BEAR		GRIZZLY BEAR
☐	Size	☐
☐	Claws	☐
☐	Hunting Skill	☐
☐	Teeth	☐
☐	Sense of Smell	☐
☐	Speed	☐
☐	Family	☐
☐	Hibernation	☐

Author note: This was one way the fight might have ended. How would you write the ending?

WHO HAS THE ADVANTAGE?
CHECKLIST

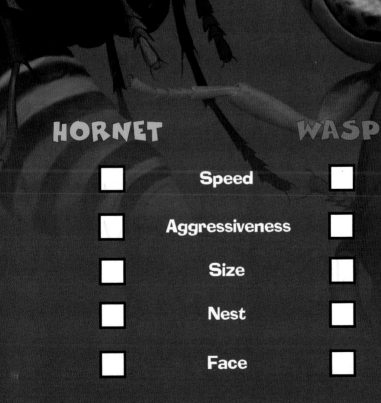

HORNET

WASP

	Speed	
	Aggressiveness	
	Size	
	Nest	
	Face	

Author note: This is one way the fight might have ended.
How would you write the ending?

WHO HAS THE ADVANTAGE? CHECKLIST

TRICERATOPS   SPINOSAURUS

TRICERATOPS		SPINOSAURUS
☐	Size	☑
☐	Speed	☑
☑	Horns	☐
☐	Claws	☐
☐	Weight	☐
☐	Armor	☐

Author's note: This is one way the fight might have ended. How would you write the ending?

WHO DO YOU THINK WOULD WIN?

KILLER WHALE VS GREAT WHITE SHARK

LION VS TIGER

POLAR BEAR VS GRIZZLY BEAR

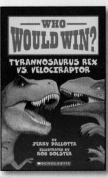

TYRANNOSAURUS REX VS. VELOCIRAPTOR

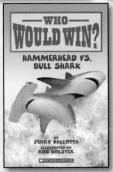

HAMMERHEAD VS. BULL SHARK

KOMODO DRAGON VS. KING COBRA

TARANTULA VS. SCORPION

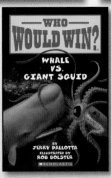

WHALE VS. GIANT SQUID

BATTLE ROYALE — 5 BOOKS IN 1!

Find out who comes out on top by reading more of these animal matchups!

WHO WOULD WIN?

ULTIMATE SHOWDOWN